4/18/03

Best wishes for creating a
change-resilient organization!

Praise for *"It" Happens!*

"This book will help you move beyond simply talking about what needs to change, to actually doing something about it. *"It" Happens!* will help you clarify the behaviors and consequences you need to bring about lasting change. This behavior-consequence connection is so important that we've made it the underpinning of our leadership curriculum at Bayer Corporation."

—JAY M. DUFFY
Director, Executive Education and Leadership
Bayer Corporation

"My organization is in the middle of a merger, with huge management turnover in my department. As new challenges are placed before me, I pick up the Change Puzzle from my desk and use each piece to help me deal with the inner conflicts I face. This wonderful book has brought me peace of mind and a healthier outlook on future challenges and change."

—CAROL MARTIN
Staffing Coordinator of Patient Services
Fairmont General Hospital

"As a leader, I not only have to propose changes, I have to rally people behind them. This is just the book I've been waiting for—a true how-to guide to help anyone successfully cope with change."

—BEVERLY A. GRANT
Director, North America MDO—
Snacks, Beverage and Pet Nutrition
The Procter & Gamble Company

"The Change Puzzle is not another flavor-of-the-month. It's one of the few tools we have used at our company where people 'get it'—not only professionally, but personally. By using the Change Puzzle, people begin to view change as an opportunity, with endless positive possibilities."

—STEVE PENDILL
Business Development Executive
Sierra Pacific Resources

"This book, *"It" Happens!,* was a real eye-opener for me. I never thought about the impact my 'Thoughts and Beliefs' had on how I dealt with change. Thanks to this book, I'm now able to reframe my negative thoughts into positive thoughts, and this really helps me deal with change in a positive way."

—SCOTT T. PALMER
Student
Sherando High School

"Change is pervasive. High-quality tools to help individuals become Change-Resilient are scarce. *"It" Happens!* gives change management consultants quality tools to support our clients through life's changes."

—SUSAN MOORE, PH.D.
Director
FLI, Incorporated

"I've been a manager at a major federal agency for over 20 years and have seen many management books come and go. *"It" Happens!* is different—it will have lasting impact. It provided me with outstanding insight into how to manage change. I feel that I can share the tools in the book with my employees and together we can handle any change more effectively."

—STEVEN D. SLAHTA
Attorney

"Dealing with change is hard human work full of complex and often conflicting emotions. Dr. Smith deals with the topic in two ways . . . first through an allegory where we are able to identify our most immediate and natural response to the changes we face, and then by providing tools we can use to actually work our way through change when it happens to and around us. Read her book once and you are likely to think that it's simple; read it again and you are likely to begin to use the change tools; add it to your library and you are likely to consult it for real-time assistance with real-time change."

—NANCY GRABLE
Former Senior Executive
Airline Industry

"I work in a hurried and taxing environment with many people who are, like myself, very stubborn. So, when we face change, whether it is a new staff member or a new protocol, our doggedness gets in the way. None of us has the time to take a class to learn how to adapt to changes. This book provides an enjoyable way for harried professionals to learn how to roll with the punches. Resilience is a critical job skill in today's workplace. If everyone on a work team reads this book, no doubt their professional relationships and overall performance will improve."

—SHANE WASLEY
Premed Student and EMT
UCLA

"This book is packed full of useful examples and practical recommendations. Dr. Smith knows her territory well and has made an invaluable contribution to understanding how winning companies manage change."

—KENT STERETT
President
Premier Performance Network

"It" Happens!

"It" Happens!

How to Become Change-Resilient

JULIE M. SMITH, PH.D.

LifePath Press

© LifePath Press 2002.

The Change Puzzle™ is a trademark of LifePath, LLC and is
based on the Breakthrough Model, © 1995 by CLG.

LifePath™ is a trademark of LifePath, LLC.
For more information on LifePath, visit
www.lifepathonline.com.

Printed in the United States of America.

LifePath Press
3315 Four H Camp Road
Morgantown, WV 26508
(304) 284-9223

ISBN 0-9721103-0-5

First Edition

10 9 8 7 6 5 4 3 2 1

Dedication

*To my husband Mickey,
my Blink, who helps me live in the moment.*

*To Lynne, my wise Sparky,
who taught me to honor the past
to create a boundless future.*

Contents

Prologue

This tale is about making yourself *CHANGE-RESILIENT* whenever *it happens.* *"It"* is any change that affects you personally, good or bad, planned or unplanned. *CHANGE-RESILIENT* means that you adjust easily with courage and confidence when *it happens.*

Some changes in life are easy to accept because we want them to happen. Other changes are unwelcome, and we resist them to the bitter end. This story will show you and others you care about an easier way to handle any change, large or small, welcome or unwelcome.

This story introduces a *Change Puzzle* and *Change Cards* you can use to guide your way through any changes you encounter. These tools are invaluable—chock-full of information distilled from decades of behavioral science research.

When *it happens* to you, the puzzle and cards will help you become more adaptable and flexible, to roll with the punches. You'll be able to not only survive a change but to thrive during the change. In short, you will become *CHANGE-RESILIENT!*

Whenever *it happens* to you, depending on what the change is, you probably react like one or more of the characters in this story:

Blink the bear, who reacts to change without analyzing—he just blinks and goes . . .

Ruff the squirrel, who resists change mightily because he is so entangled in his negative feelings, thoughts, and beliefs . . .

Rosie the squirrel, who is receptive to change but struggles because she doesn't know how to plan and follow through . . .

Ebb and Flo, resilient people who use the Change Puzzle to handle change as it unfolds and show others the way . . .

And *Sparky*, who is the master of **CHANGE-RESILIENCE,** reacting to change with courage and confidence and proactively creating change.

Join me now on this short adventure in the forest . . . an adventure during which you watch Ruff and Rosie learn to become **CHANGE-RESILIENT** . . .

Note: Some people love nothing more than a good story, especially if it imparts pearls of wisdom that are revealed as the tale unfolds. Others prefer the storyteller to get right to the point. This book hopefully will satisfy both kinds of people. If stories appeal to you, proceed to Chapter 1 to meet the cast of characters. If you favor getting to the facts, skip to the section entitled, *Pulling "It" All Together* (see page 103). It will guide you through how to use the Change Puzzle and Change Puzzle Cards.

CHAPTER ONE

"It" Happens!

Two squirrels stood in the mouth of a cave in a smoldering forest, calling after a bear named Blink, who lumbered down the path.

"Blink, stop!" cried Ruff as he wiped a tear from his eye. "The fire destroyed all our Treasures! Everything we value! Our food, our home, our safety!"

"What should we do?" asked Rosie, the more practical of the two.

"Move on," the bear shrugged.

"But where?" Rosie asked.

"Across Rushing River. To the forest called New World. I bet it's still there," Blink said. "I doubt the fire jumped the river. Let's go."

"But we can't just pick up and leave," Ruff protested, catching up with Blink. "This is home!"

"When *it happens*," Blink said, "when your old world burns down, you gotta go out and find a new one."

"Not yet!" Ruff wailed and tugged on Blink's tail to hold him back. But the great bear walked on, dragging the grief-stricken squirrel behind.

"Look," Blink said. "Whenever *it happens*, I just blink and go. Go with your gut, Ruff! Use your instincts!"

But Ruff was frozen, devastated—too heartbroken to do anything. All he could do was mutter angrily, "People caused this fire. You can bet your life on that."

"I think we should go," said Rosie, hurrying to her friend. But Ruff sat down again at the side of the trail and buried his head in his paws. Rosie laid a gentle paw on Ruff's shoulder, then turned to see Blink disappear over a blackened hill far in the distance, straight toward whatever lay ahead.

She knew she should go too. But how could she leave Ruff behind?

CHAPTER TWO

Ruff and Rosie
Meet Ebb and Flo

The next morning found Ruff sitting at the mouth of the cave and Rosie standing over him, gesturing wildly. "We can't just sit here and do nothing, Ruff! I know you're hurt. I know you're sad—"

Ruff snarled. "Why can't people be careful with fire!"

"I don't know," said Rosie. "But we've got to do something. If we stay here we'll die!"

"Why bother doing anything?" said Ruff. "We're doomed."

"Maybe not, Ruff. If we go to New World . . ."

"No!" Ruff exclaimed. "New World won't have the Treasures we want."

"Ruff, try to look on the bright side," she replied. "Maybe things will grow back! I mean that's what forests do, right?"

Suddenly a shadow fell over them. "What next?" Ruff sighed. "Now the sky's falling, I suppose."

When he and Rosie looked up, they saw a silver-haired couple staring down at them—a man and woman in hiking outfits wearing puzzled expressions on their faces. They looked as if they'd never seen talking squirrels before.

"Are . . . uhm . . . you two all right?" the woman asked. "Was somebody singed in that terrible fire?"

"PEOPLE!" screamed Ruff. "Run for your life!"

Rosie began to run in frantic circles, screaming and chirping in terror. And when Ruff stared into the eyes of the two giants looming over him, he fainted dead away.

"Oh my," said the woman.

"Don't be afraid," said the man to Rosie. "I'm Ebenezer and this is my wife, Flora. You can call us Ebb and Flo."

The woman took Ruff's paw carefully between her fingers and patted it, trying to revive the little creature. "There, there," said Flo. "You two are going to be just fine."

"You burned down Old World!" yelled Rosie as she continued to run in circles.

The man reached out and deftly grabbed Rosie as she hurtled by. Lifting the little squirrel by the scruff of her neck, Ebb looked into her eyes as Rosie kicked and squirmed.

"We didn't burn Old World," Ebb said. "A bolt of *lightning* started the fire."

"That fire must have been frightening for you," Flo said as she helped Ruff to his feet.

"It was," said Rosie, who couldn't quite believe she had found the courage to talk to a human being. "It destroyed everything we've ever known or loved. All our Treasures."

"That's terrible," said Flo. "But maybe Ebb and I can help you and your friend find new Treasures."

"Flo?" said Ebb. "We've got our own problems to solve."

"No one can help us," sighed Ruff, too stunned to do anything but allow the woman to help him to his feet.

"When your old world burns down," said Flo, frowning at her husband, "sometimes you need a friend or two to help you get back on your feet."

"We're headed to see just such a friend," said Ebb, frowning right back in an effort to convince Flo that they should leave these squirrels to their own devices and hurry down the path.

But Flo would not be moved. "When we were in trouble, a friend helped us," said Flo. "And all he asked in return was that we 'pay it forward,' as the saying goes."

"You're right," conceded Ebb. He touched a shiny key that hung from his belt. "Our friend Sparky gave us the key to handling change whenever *it happens.*"

Flo nodded in agreement and clutched a similar key that hung from the chain around her neck.

"But if you've got the keys to handling change already," asked Rosie, "what do you need to see this 'Sparky' for?"

"Well," said Ebb as he placed Rosie on the ground, "a major event has happened in our lives too, and for some reason we're stuck."

Flo explained, "Ebb works for an educational software company. It's been bought out—"

"—by a multinational entertainment conglomerate from overseas," said Ebb.

"Conglomerate?" said Ruff.

"It's a big . . . never mind," Ebb said. "The point is, I'm worried about the changes they want to make."

"I don't see how some of the video games they develop have anything to do with education," Flo added. *"Kidnap and Murder II?* I mean, really! Ebb's got a very good reputation in the industry—"

"They've asked me to stay on," Ebb added. "But I'm not sure. I'm not getting any younger. I could retire if I wanted to."

"So you've got a big decision to make too," said Rosie.

"By the end of the week," said Ebb. "So we're going to visit my old boss Sparky, who hired me right out of school. He's sort of my mentor. I want to talk to him before I decide."

"He's retired to a cabin on the other side of Rushing River," said Flo.

Ebb grinned. "Guy ties flies all day. I don't know if I'm ready for that."

"Ties flies? It's next to impossible to catch one," argued Ruff, "and you're telling me this Sparky ties 'em up!"

"My name's Rosie, by the way," interrupted the other squirrel. "And that's my best friend, Ruff."

"It's nice to meet you, Ruff and Rosie," said Ebb.

"Whatever," groused Ruff, eyeing the man suspiciously.

"It's nice to meet you too, Ebb and Flo," said Rosie as she stepped between Ruff and the silver-haired gentleman. "You'll have to excuse my friend. Ruff hasn't quite been himself since our forest burned down."

"That kind of loss—that type of change—can really throw a person for a loop," said Ebb.

"Not to mention squirrels," Ruff replied contemptuously.

"But when you learn the keys to handling change," offered Flo, "your life becomes filled with new opportunities."

"Sounds interesting," said Rosie. "Huh, Ruff?"

Ruff looked at the couple who stood just outside the mouth of the cave. He leaned over to Rosie and whispered, "Rosie, they're people. You can't believe a word they say. Tying flies? Come on, the man's a bald-faced liar!"

"But she says they know how to handle change!" Rosie replied. "They know how to find new Treasures!"

"If they know so much, why are they going to visit this guy named Sparky?"

"Look, I'm ready to go to New World right now! But I need you to go with me!"

"Rosie, I'm not feeling very well," Ruff replied.

"You just fainted. You'll be fine."

"I did not faint! That guy kicked me in the head or something. I can't leave yet. Not 'til I'm feeling better."

Flo held out the golden key from around her neck. It shone brightly, even in the half-light of the cave. She stepped toward Ruff and Rosie and dangled the key over Ruff's pink nose. He sniffed it curiously.

"You see my Change Key, Ruff?" Flo asked. "I use it to stay open to life's changes."

"Bunk," Ruff snorted.

"A key like that can help you and Rosie unlock yourselves, so you can be open to new things," said Ebb.

The squirrels studied the Change Key. They read the words inscribed on one side: **BE CHANGE-RESILIENT!**

"What does *Change-Resilient* mean?" Rosie asked.

CHAPTER THREE

Ebb and Flo Explain "Change-Resilient"

"Change-Resilient means that you adjust easily with courage and confidence when it happens," Flo said.

"Whenever I feel myself resisting change or getting scared," said Ebb, "like I am now with this merger, I touch my Change Key. It reminds me to be open to what's happened and what's going to happen."

Rosie grew excited. All of a sudden she felt hopeful. "And you say you get those keys from your friend Sparky?"

"Yep. Sparky taught us, step-by-step, how to become Change-Resilient," Ebb said. "And I know we could teach you what he taught us."

"I don't think so," Ruff grumped.

"If you become Change-Resilient, you'll become happier," said Ebb, who offered his key to the wary squirrel. "Tell you what, Ruff. Flo has her Change Key . . . so maybe you and Rosie could use mine until I can get to Sparky's for another."

"Ebb?" Flo asked. "Are you sure?"

The gentleman nodded. "That's very generous of you," said Rosie. "Isn't it, Ruff?"

Mesmerized by the shiny object, Ruff reached for Ebb's key.

When he took it in his paw, something strange and mysterious happened. Suddenly, Ruff felt off-balance and lightheaded. Everything he had heard about people—that they were dangerous, that they could never be trusted—was being challenged by Ebb and Flo.

Could he be mistaken about New World too? Ruff's head swam. He wasn't sure what he believed anymore.

CHAPTER FOUR

The Advantages of Being Change-Resilient

When Ruff snapped out of his trance, he discovered Rosie sitting between Ebb and Flo, eating peanuts from Flo's knapsack. Rosie and the couple were laughing about something.

"Oh yes!" said Flo. "Without so much as a phone call, mind you. Can you imagine?"

Ruff looked down to discover that he was still grasping Ebb's Change Key in his paw.

"And the first thing out of Ebb's mouth," Flo continued, "isn't how sorry he is for surprising me like that—bringing his boss home for supper without the least bit of warning. No! The first thing out of Ebb's mouth is how much he admires Sparky for his ability to handle change!"

"That was the night Sparky gave Flo her Change Key," Ebb said.

"And boy did I need it," said Flo. "I wasn't expecting guests, you see."

Ebb chuckled. "But Sparky handed Flo her key, asked if he could make a salad, and said, 'It pays to be resilient because *change is an inevitable part of life.*'"

"Sparky taught us a lot of things that night," said Flo. "He showed us how change can be small, like a sudden change in dinner plans or getting sick at your daughter's wedding."

Ebb grimaced and said, "I'd rather not talk about that."

"Or the change can be big, like your company being bought out."

"I don't know if I wanna talk about that now either," Ebb replied.

"Or," Flo lowered her head and said quietly, "It can be traumatic, like a child dies and you suffer through a spiritual crisis because you're not sure what you believe in anymore."

She and Ebb looked sadly at each other for a long moment until Rosie spoke to break the silence. "Or you have to move," she offered cautiously.

"Exactly," said Ebb, thankful that the squirrel had pulled him out of his thoughts. "The change can be expected or unexpected, welcome or unwelcome, planned or unplanned, caused by nature or by people."

Flo added, "And it can be under your control or out of it."

"That's the kind I really hate. The kind that's out of my control," said Rosie.

"Me too," sighed Flo.

"Me too!" chirped Ruff, trying to join in. "That kind is . . . complicated!"

"They all can be," said Flo. "Even the changes you've planned and are looking forward to—like the birth of a new baby. That's why so many folks have so much trouble with change, Ruff. But it doesn't have to be hard all the time."

"It all depends on how you handle *it,*" said Ebb. "Sparky taught us that we react to change in three different ways. We are either . . ." and he picked up a stick and wrote in the dust:

- Resistant—we ignore <u>it</u> or kick and scream
- Receptive—we accept <u>it</u> or embrace <u>it</u>, but our good intentions don't result in positive action
- Resilient—we adjust easily with courage and confidence when <u>it happens</u>

"I think I'm the type who is receptive to change," Rosie said.

"Me too," said Ruff.

"Who are you trying to kid?" said Rosie. "You're a kicker and a screamer if ever there was one!"

"Well, if I kick and scream, it's because I hate change so much!" Ruff said defensively.

"Maybe, Ruff," Ebb continued, "you can find a more positive way to react."

"I react how I react," said Ruff curtly.

"Sure you do," said Ebb. "But you could learn to control how you respond. After all, the quality of our lives is determined not by what happens to us but by how we handle *it* when it happens."

"When you become Change-Resilient," he continued, "your life will improve in four wonderful ways. You will be able to . . ." and he wrote in the dust:

- Handle any change, even a crisis
- Move forward—get past fear, unlock, and open yourself to opportunities
- Find the Treasures that are always hidden or unexpected in any change
- Improve the overall quality of your life

Flo looked at Ruff. "What do you think?"

Ruff stepped from the cave. "I suppose it makes sense," he offered.

"Progress!" Ebb exclaimed. "It does make sense! Good work, Ruff!"

"Hey, progress isn't easy when you're going through a change!" Ruff grumped. "'Cause you feel trapped and hissed. Frozen, like Rushing River in January."

"It's as human as human to be frozen and afraid in the face of change," said Flo.

"Hey, I'm not a human. I'm a squirrel. And I didn't say I was afraid. I said I was hissed."

Rosie cocked an eyebrow and asked, "Ruff, what in the world do you mean by 'hissed'?"

The question irritated Ruff, because he wasn't sure what he meant. He replied, "I dunno. But anyway, don't worry, I'm over it now."

"Good!" Ebb said, "Then you're ready to go!"

"Where?"

"To New World. 'Cause Flo and I need to get to Sparky's, remember?"

"I . . . uhm . . . I can't just yet. Me and Rosie have a few things we need to wrap up here first. Right, Roe?"

Rosie looked to Ebb and Flo for help.

"Change Puzzle!" they said at exactly the same time, as only couples who've been together forever can do.

CHAPTER FIVE

The Change Puzzle

Ebb and Flo fished in their coat pockets. Each pulled out a small, brightly colored puzzle cube with words printed on the sides. Ebb held his up for Rosie to inspect. And Flo did the same for Ruff.

Ebb and Flo turned the puzzles over in their hands so that Ruff and Rosie could read the words printed on the sides. Then, suddenly, Ebb and Flo tossed the puzzles to the ground. When they hit, the puzzles popped apart and the pieces scattered in the dust.

"Wha'd you do that for?!" cried Ruff. "Now we'll have to put 'em back together!"

"Don't you see, we're supposed to!" sang Rosie. "They're Change Puzzles. Putting them back together will help us learn how to become Change-Resilient."

"That's right," said Flo, pulling a stack of cards from her backpack. "Working this puzzle will help you handle any change that comes your way. Each piece represents a very important step in dealing with change. Sparky gave us these cards to remind us how to use the puzzle."

Flo carefully untied the ribbon that held the worn cards together. She showed the squirrels what was on the first card.

The Change Puzzle Pieces

1. **"It" Happens!** is any change that affects me. It can be expected or unexpected, welcome or unwelcome, planned or unplanned, under my control or out of it, caused by nature or by people.

2. **My Feelings** are the emotions I experience when going through a change.

3. **My Thoughts & Beliefs**—thoughts are ideas that run through my head about the change. They are private and known only to me. Beliefs are opinions that I hold deep inside as absolute truths.

4. **My Behaviors** are everything I say or do when I am affected by a change.

5. **Consequences to Me** are things that occur after my behaviors and either encourage or discourage me from doing the same behaviors again.

6. **My Impact on Others** is about the effect my behaviors have on others.

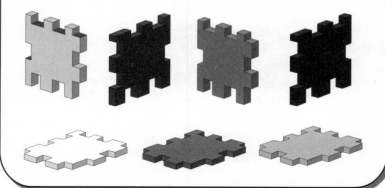

CHAPTER SIX

Piecing Together the Change Puzzle

"So there you have the Change Puzzle!" Flo said. "Any questions?"

"Yeah, I have a question!" Ruff groused.

"How can I tell if I put my Change Puzzle together right?"

"There is only one way to tell if you've put your puzzle together in the right way," said Flo. *"When a change happens, you must fit together all six pieces of the puzzle in a way that you can be proud of."*

"If you put together your Change Puzzle in a way that's right for you, you'll be able to honestly answer **YES!** to all of these questions," said Flo as she pulled another card from the stack.

"The meter shows you where you are—whether you are resistant, receptive, or resilient toward change."

My Change-Resilience Meter

	Yes	No	Unsure
1. Am I proud of how I'm handling this **"It"?**	❏	❏	❏
2. Are **My Feelings** about the change positive?	❏	❏	❏
3. Are **My Thoughts & Beliefs** about the change positive?	❏	❏	❏
4. Am I proud of **My Behaviors?** · Am I doing things I feel good about? · Am I doing things I believe in? · Am I doing things that help me move forward?	❏	❏	❏
5. Are the **Consequences to Me** encouraging my positive behaviors?	❏	❏	❏
6. Is **My Impact on Others** positive, especially people I care about?	❏	❏	❏

No to questions 2 or 3

Yes to 2 & 3; No to 1, 4, 5, or 6

Yes to all questions

I'M RESISTANT   **I'M RECEPTIVE**   **I'M RESILIENT**

If I checked "no" or "unsure" to any question, I should continue to work the Change Puzzle pieces until I can honestly answer "yes."

Rosie asked the next question.

"Can I force a piece to fit into my Change Puzzle?"

"No," said Flo. "Never force anything. If you have to force a puzzle piece, that means something else isn't right.

"For example, if you can't get your *My Impact on Others* piece to fit, it might be because your *Behaviors* piece is in wrong—so the things you are saying or doing might be having a negative effect on others."

"Don't worry," Ebb said. "You'll be able to tell if you are forcing a piece because you won't feel proud of how you've assembled the cube. And you won't be able to answer **YES!** to all of the questions listed on the card."

It was Ruff's turn.

"In what order do I work my Change Puzzle pieces?"

"Always start with the piece called ***"It" Happens!"*** Flo said. "Here's why: *it is any change that affects you,* so when *it* **happens**, it's the trigger for using your Change Puzzle."

"I see!" said Ruff. "My *it* was the fire, which took away my Treasures!"

"Yes," Flo said. "Starting with *"It" Happens!*, you can assemble the puzzle pieces in any order."

"Some people like to work the puzzle in the same order every time. For instance, some believe that they have to change their beliefs first and then their behaviors will change. Others try new behaviors first, and that causes their beliefs to change."

"In real life, how you respond to a change won't always be in an orderly fashion," said Ebb. "But as you become more skilled at using the puzzle, you'll learn how best to sequence the pieces for yourself."

"For now," said Flo, "we'll look at the puzzle pieces in a certain order because it's easier to learn the puzzle that way."

Rosie frowned.

"If it's really hard to get one of the pieces to fit, like My Feelings, can I just leave it out?"

"No!" Ebb laughed. "You'd only be cheating yourself! You can't leave out any pieces, especially the ones that you don't want to deal with!"

"If you try to short-circuit the process, it may backfire on you," said Flo. "I've seen people move to action immediately after a change hits them. But they later get depressed and can't get out of bed because they never dealt with their emotions."

"There is a purpose for every piece, and there is something to learn from every one. If you skip a piece, you can't become truly Change-Resilient."

Ruff had one more question.

"Once I put my puzzle together for a change, will I ever have to redo it?"

"It depends," Ebb said. "As you puzzle through a change, you may have to rework the pieces as you learn new things about yourself.

"Say you try a new behavior, like going to New World to search for Treasures. Your thoughts might change about what you consider to be a Treasure once you get there."

CHAPTER SEVEN

Ruff and Rosie See the Power of the Puzzle

Rosie let out a low whistle. "This is important stuff!"

Ruff suddenly smiled. "Wait a minute!" he said. "You mean to tell me—if I learn how to use this Change Puzzle, I can get my old life back?"

"No, Ruff," Ebb said quietly. "We don't mean that at all. When *it happens*, everything changes. As much as you'd like, you can never go back to the way it used to be."

"Like when we lost our son," Flo said. "Oh, how I wanted him back."

Ebb couldn't make eye contact with Flo as he considered her words. He sighed heavily and said, "Me too," his eyes filling with tears. "That loss took a long time for me to accept."

"Sometimes handling change means you have to grieve for quite a while," said Flo.

"But Sparky helped us see that you can get frozen in your grief," said Ebb. "Our other children needed us. That time, the Change Puzzle saved our family."

"Losing our home can't come close to losing a child," Ruff said quietly.

"It was the worst thing that's ever happened to us," Flo said softly. "I thought we'd never be happy again. It took a long time to work our way through all the puzzle pieces."

The foursome sat silently, thinking about all the turmoil change brings.

Ebb broke the silence. "Would you two like to learn to use the Change Puzzle?" he said. "'Cause Flo and I can teach you how to use it to work through your situation."

The two squirrels looked at one another. Rosie said, "I do!" just as Ruff knew she would.

"You sure there's no going back?" Ruff asked.

"I'm afraid not," Flo replied.

"Then I guess I better learn," he said.

"Good," said Flo. "Keep this in mind, Ruff. The Change Puzzle will help you find new Treasures that are not apparent to you yet—because this is a new situation for you.

"You need to be open to whatever might happen. Only then can you find these hidden Treasures."

Ruff stood and brushed the dust off his tail. "All right," he said with grim determination. "Where do we begin?"

"Ruff!" Rosie cried. "I knew you had it in you."

"We all do," said Ebb, as he patted the little guy on the shoulder. "And you know, Ruff, working on the Change Puzzle with you and Rosie might help Flo and me decide whether it's going to be merger or retirement."

"Where do we start?" asked Ruff.

"Flo says always start with the *"It" Happens!* piece, remember?" Rosie said. "Then we go to *My Behaviors,* I guess."

"Not yet, Rosie," Flo replied. "You're flexible by nature, somewhat open to change, so you've already worked two puzzle pieces on your own."

"I have?" Rosie gasped.

"Yes," said Ebb, "you have. *My Feelings* and *My Thoughts & Beliefs.* So you're receptive to change and anxious to move on to *My Behaviors.* You're anxious to get going. But Ruff's not there yet."

"Yeah, Rosie," Ruff said. "Give me a break. I gotta puzzle through some feelings first."

"You've gotta puzzle through some thoughts and beliefs too, pal," Rosie said smugly.

"Now, Rosie," Flo cautioned, "Ruff doesn't have to do anything he doesn't want to. But working those pieces of the puzzle could help."

"Why don't we all start with the *My Feelings* piece?" said Ebb. "I could use the opportunity to take inventory of my feelings."

"Really, Ebb?" Ruff asked.

"Sure. Especially after this takeover business," said Ebb. "Okay. What're my feelings about working for my new boss? **Conflicted** to say the least."

"Be specific, dear," said Flo.

"A bit **frightened**, I guess," said Ebb. "And **worried** that the company I've given my life to is gonna focus on making video games that dull kids' senses rather than stimulate them. I'm **ambivalent** about retirement. I'm 57 years old; I'm not getting any younger. But I'm not dead yet either! And I'm **resentful** that by retiring I might give people the impression that I quit. I've always been **committed** to the company. And the one thing I'm not is a quitter."

"I understand how you feel, dear," Flo encouraged.

"How 'bout you, Ruff," Ebb asked. "What're your feelings?"

CHAPTER EIGHT

"My Feelings" Puzzle Piece

"My Feelings?" Ruff said, as he turned the piece over and over in his paws. "Good question."

"You know, Ruff," Ebb replied, "feelings are the emotions you experience when you're going through a change."

"I know that," the squirrel said defensively.

"It's helpful to look at your feelings first, Ruff," said Flo, "because they're usually the first response you have to change. They're right in your gut, like the instant fear that comes over you when you find yourself in crisis."

"And those fears can make other pieces of the puzzle pop apart," said Ebb. "Fear can cause your thoughts to spin out of control and make you say and do things you regret."

"Look," snapped Ruff, "I already know I'm hissed about what happened! What else is there to know?"

"Well," Flo replied, "feelings aren't always simple. Usually, you have more than one feeling about a change. More than just being hissed."

"And sometimes you might even have feelings that are at odds with one another," said Ebb, "so that you become conflicted without even knowing it."

"The first step is to untangle them so you're aware of *all* your feelings about a change: good and bad, happy and sad," said Flo. "Like Ebb just did."

"I don't like talking about feelings. I'm not into that touchy-feely stuff," said Ruff, tossing the puzzle piece to the ground.

"How can somebody like Ruff, who hates to deal with his feelings, begin to untangle them?" Rosie asked.

"Well, Ruff can listen to his body," Flo said. "Our bodies give us direct signals all the time about how we're feeling."

"For example," Ebb added, "your heart may speed up, or your stomach may tighten into a knot—"

"Or your paws might sweat!" chirped Ruff.

"That's right! And you might feel lightheaded and confused," added Ebb. "Those're all signs that you might be *frightened.*"

"Or, on the positive side," Flo added, "you may feel a sudden burst of energy even though you're tired. That could be a sign you're excited about some aspect of the change."

"Your body also might send signals indirectly of how you are feeling," Flo continued. "Sometimes when we don't know how we're feeling, it shows up anyway in our body language—like frowning without knowing it."

"I think I'm open about my feelings," said Rosie. "Even though I know it makes Ruff squirm, I talk about my feelings all the time. Like I'll say, 'I'm scared,' or 'I'm confused,' or 'I'm sad.' That's what I did after the fire."

"You're very lucky, being like that," said Flo, "because a squirrel can become aware of her feelings just by naming them."

"But it helps if the names you use are clear," said Ebb. "What do you mean when you say you're 'hissed,' Ruff?"

"Yeah," Rosie said. "What do you mean by that?"

"You know . . . uhm . . . hissed," replied Ruff. "When your hair stands up and you show all your teeth. Don't you get hissed sometimes, Ebb?"

"Well, I show my teeth when I smile," Ebb offered. "Is that what you mean?"

"No! You know . . . hissed!—Oh! I don't know, I don't know how to name my feelings. I'm a squirrel! It's not like I have a college degree!"

"It's not about how many years you went to school," Flo said calmly. "It's not about your job title or where you live. It's about whether you've learned to identify your feelings."

"Here," said Ebb. "Here's a card that might help you. It has words Flo and I use to describe our feelings. See a word that might mean hissed?"

Ruff and Rosie took the card and studied it.

"The words on the left describe feelings that signal you're locked and resistant to the change," explained Ebb. "The words on the right describe feelings that signal you're unlocked and receptive to the change."

My Feelings
Change Puzzle Card

These keep me **locked**	These help me **unlock**
· Fearful	· Courageous and confident
· Resentful	· Appreciative, accepting
· Angry	· Calm, determined
· Sad	· Happy, joyful
· Guilty, embarrassed, ashamed	· Proud, worthy
· Depressed, lethargic	· Excited, energetic
· Helpless, powerless	· Confident, capable, powerful
· Ambivalent, confused	· Committed, focused
· Trapped	· Liberated
· Anxious, worried	· Relaxed
· Hopeless	· Hopeful
· Judgmental	· Empathetic
· Apathetic	· Curious
· (Add my own)	· (Add my own)

Become Aware, Then Share

"Anger!" Ruff chirped. "That's what I mean by hissed! But hey," he added, "I don't see what's wrong with being angry. Sometimes being angry about something gets you to change it."

"Good, Ruff," said Flo. "Anger can be channeled toward positive results, whatever they may be. But if your anger keeps you locked up and bitter, that's no way to live.

"The big arrow here on the card," she pointed, "suggests that you want to move from feelings on the left—like anger, which can keep you locked—to feelings on the right, like calm or determined, which help you unlock."

"Okay. But you should put anger at the top of the list," said Ruff, "because that's the emotion I always feel first."

"Really?" said Flo. "Because we've discovered that the first feeling that keeps most people locked is fear."

"I don't buy it. And anyway, squirrels are different from people," Ruff insisted. "At least I am. I'm not afraid of anything."

"Remember, there's a big mix of feelings, Ruff," Ebb offered. **"Fear** usually is at the center of all the ones that keep you locked. You might experience another feeling first, but when you scratch the surface, fear is usually underneath."

"Not me," said Ruff stubbornly.

"Take my situation," said Ebb. "When I heard about the merger, I was really angry about potentially losing my job—"

Suddenly he stopped and wiped the palms of his hands on his trousers. "I can't believe it," he said, surprised by the depth of his own feeling. "I'm sweating just talking about it."

"Here Ebb," Flo said. "Touch the key."

He reached out and touched the Change Key that hung from her neck. "Gee," he said. "I had no idea I was so afraid of all this."

"Of what?" she prompted.

"That I'll have to start all over again at my age. That I won't be respected for my expertise."

"And?" she offered again.

"And that I won't be able to hold my temper in front of the man who just 'right-sized' about thirty of my friends."

Flo looked at Ruff. "Now that Ebb's aware of his underlying fears, he'll be able to deal with them. Right, Ebb?"

Ruff frowned, not convinced.

Ebb paused to think about Flo's question. "It's been hard," he said. "But I've learned it's very important to face your fears when *it happens*, Ruff. You can't be afraid to say you're afraid."

Flo smiled at Ruff. "The tip shown at the bottom of the card—***Become Aware, Then Share***—is a valuable lesson for unlocking our feelings," she said.

"So if I've got this right . . ." said Ruff, " . . . first, become aware of your feelings. Then, once you're aware of them, share them with someone else."

"Yes," answered Flo. "Don't just look for someone to commiserate with or you'll stay stuck in negativity. Look for someone who is nonjudgmental and a good listener, someone who can help you move on in spite of your fears."

"Ruff," Ebb confessed, "I used to keep my negative feelings locked up inside—what a mistake! But when I share them with Flo, who's naturally better with change than I am, I'm always able to unlock and let go."

"Now, Ruff," Flo asked. "Do you think you can make the *My Feelings* piece fit with the ***"It" Happens!*** piece?"

Ruff picked up the piece he had flung to the ground, then tried connecting it to ***"It" Happens!*** "So this is it, huh. This is where I've got to share my feelings about losing Old World to the fire?"

"Yep," said Ebb.

"Well," said the squirrel, "I felt scared. Full of fear. I'll admit it. And sad. And angry." He thought hard for a while, then looked at the card. "And I felt resentful. And helpless. And trapped. Just about every emotion on the negative side of the card!"

Rosie abruptly put her paws on her haunches and declared, "Well, why didn't you tell me in the first place? Then maybe I could've helped you!"

"'Cause I was blocked, Rosie! Duh!" Ruff stopped and composed himself. "I'm sorry, Rosie. I know you wanted to help. But I didn't know *how* to say what I felt."

"I'm sorry too," said Rosie, a bit chagrined. "I appreciate you sharing your feelings now."

"It hasn't been easy," he said, "but I feel a lot better."

"That's great!" exclaimed Ebb and Flo.

"And I want to share something else," Ruff added. "Even though I have a long list of negative feelings that lock me up, I do have a positive one. I actually feel *curious* about what Treasures might be in New World."

"Wonderful!" Ebb said. "You can use a positive feeling like that to unlock!"

"So can you," said Flo.

"Okay," Ebb said. "I do feel somewhat optimistic. I think I can use my seniority and influence to make sure that the important aspects of the old company carry over to the new one."

"Okay, so now that Ebb knows what his feelings are," asked Ruff. "How does he change them?"

"By changing his thoughts and beliefs," Flo said. "And that's the next piece of the puzzle."

CHAPTER NINE

"My Thoughts & Beliefs" Puzzle Piece

"What are my thoughts and beliefs, anyhow?" asked Ruff, as he looked at the couple, who had terrified him only an hour ago.

"Your *thoughts* are ideas that run through your head, that help you make sense of things when *it happens,*" Ebb said. "And your *beliefs* are opinions that you hold deep inside as absolute truths."

"I'm having trouble connecting these two pieces, *My Thoughts & Beliefs* and *My Feelings,*" said Ruff, huffing and puffing as he struggled. "My paws must be too small!"

"Sometimes it's difficult because change can challenge your thoughts and beliefs," said Flo.

"You know, I'm having trouble connecting that piece too," Ebb said. "When my new boss asked me to stay on board, I had a lot of negative thoughts and beliefs that kept me from saying 'yes.' Still do.

"I mean, the man doesn't know me. I don't think he can appreciate me for who I am or what I can do for the company, and you know he's gonna rely on the people he knows."

"I don't see how that relates to Rosie and me," said Ruff.

"Ruff," said Ebb. "You and Rosie have some thoughts and beliefs about what things will be like in New World. For example, Rosie thinks it will be better than here, but you don't share that view. Maybe you should examine your thoughts.

"To get started, you can use this card for *My Thoughts & Beliefs.* It's just like the one for *My Feelings.*"

My Thoughts & Beliefs
Change Puzzle Card

These keep me **locked**	These help me **unlock**
· I don't believe that anything positive will come from this	· I have faith that positive things will result from this
· I'll never be able to do this	· I am competent and will be able to do this
· My fears will conquer me	· I can handle this in spite of my fears. I can conquer my fears
· I am stuck here	· I have endless choices
· No one will help me	· Others will be supportive
· I don't deserve good things	· I deserve good things
· I can't count on myself to carry through	· I can accomplish what I set out to do
· Bad things will happen	· Good things will happen
· I will never be able to replace my Treasures	· I'll be able to find the hidden Treasures that are not yet apparent
· (Add my own)	· (Add my own)

Aim to Reframe
(Think positive thoughts; test my negative thoughts)

Both squirrels studied the card. Ruff was dismayed to read many of the negative words he had been speaking ever since Old World burned down.

"I'm just a ball of negativity," Ruff said glumly.

"Right now I think I am too," agreed Ebb.

"But you know that can change, Ebb," Flo replied. "If you *reframe*—if you *rethink your negative thoughts and beliefs into positive ones.*"

"Let's say I don't think my boss will appreciate me," Ebb said, sitting next to Ruff. "I can reframe that negative thought this way: My boss will appreciate me when I show him the quality of work my team can produce."

"Reframing can be quite empowering," Flo added.

"Look at the tip on the bottom of the card—*Aim to Reframe,*" said Ebb. "Remember that the aim is always to reframe your negative thoughts and beliefs into positive ones, to see the opportunities that are embedded in every change.

"Two things help with reframing. First, **think positive thoughts.** When negative thoughts start racing through our heads, we just *stop* thinking for a second!

"Then," Ebb continued, "we tell ourselves to switch to positive thoughts, like those listed on the right-hand side of the card. We call this 'positive self-talk.' If you do this enough, positive thoughts will start to come automatically."

"If thinking positive thoughts doesn't work," said Flo, "the second way to reframe is to *test my negative thoughts*. Ebb and I do that by jumping into a situation to see if it's as bad as we thought. Or we talk with others who think and act differently from us. Maybe they see the change as an opportunity."

"Either way, we see if our negative thoughts hold true," said Ebb.

Flo turned to Ruff and Rosie. "Now, testing negative thoughts—and especially negative beliefs—takes a bit of courage. But courage is the best remedy for fear and negativity.

"Ruff, let's use the card to reframe your negative thoughts and help you unlock some more."

"Start with some of the thoughts you have about New World," said Ebb.

Ruff frowned. "Well, I mean, I know I'm not supposed to be negative. I get that much. But I still don't see how we're going to be able to make it there when we don't know a living soul.

"We don't know where the food is. And we don't know how the other squirrels do things—the 'rules of the game,' so to speak. We're gonna fall flat on our faces."

"So how can we help you reframe your thoughts to see that good things can happen there too?" asked Flo.

"*Test them* is one way to reframe," said Rosie.

"So, test them, then," said Flo.

"Okay," said Ruff. "Do we know anyone in New World? No."

"But we do," said, Rosie. "Blink's there. We know Blink."

"Yeah, but . . . but we don't know where any food is!" replied Ruff forcefully.

"Sure we do," said Rosie. "Acorns are in the oak trees and berries are in the bramble bushes."

"Okay, fine, but we don't know the rules," said Ruff, a bit less forcefully. "Do we?"

"Well, I know one rule. My brother taught it to me. When you move to a new neighborhood, it's up to you to introduce yourself because most squirrels are too busy to introduce themselves."

"Oh," said Ruff, realizing that each of the thoughts he'd had about New World was untrue. Then, all of a sudden, he realized something quite useful. He realized how he might be able to fit the first three pieces of the puzzle together.

"Holy smoke!" he exclaimed. "I could use my feeling of curiosity to find out what New World is really like. And once I get there, my thoughts and beliefs will be based on what's really real, not just on what's in my head."

"Very good, Ruff," Flo responded.

"And once we're there, we'll teach you how to work the other puzzle pieces," encouraged Ebb. "Right now, Ruff, you just need to be willing to go!"

"N-n-now?" stammered Ruff.

"Repeat after me," Flo said. "I CAN CONQUER MY FEARS!"

"I c-c-can conquer my f-fears," he stammered.

"C'mon, Ruff!" Rosie encouraged. "Are you willing to go or not? Tell me you can conquer your fears! Come on!"

"I can conquer my f-fears!"

"Keep thinking that, Ruff! Keep believing!" encouraged Flo.

"I *can* conquer my fears!" he said. "I can. And I *deserve* good things. And I *will* be able to find new Treasures! I know it!"

"Does that mean you'll go?" asked Rosie, waiting breathlessly for the answer.

Ruff looked at her. Then he looked at Ebb, then at Flo. "Yes!" said Ruff. "Let's do it!"

"Hooray!" the others shouted.

But almost as an omen to warn everyone that change is never easy, lightning flickered and thunder clapped far in the distance.

CHAPTER TEN

Crossing into New World

The storm began. The wind blew and the rain poured down as the foursome hurried along the riverbank toward a fallen tree that bridged Rushing River. The tree was their way across. Suddenly they stopped and watched the tree-bridge break loose, swept away in the river's raging waters.

"Oh, no!" Rosie cried.

"The bridge is gone!" Ruff wailed. "We'll never get across to New World now! This just isn't meant to be!"

"Take heart!" Ebb hollered. "And keep thinking *positively!* We *will* find a way!"

"First, we need shelter!" Flo declared, pulling an umbrella from her backpack. Ebb did the same, and the four huddled under a tiny canopy of twin umbrellas.

By now, Ruff was trembling and crying again, and Rosie looked defeated too, ready to turn back. "Come on, guys!" said Ebb. "Here's the *My Thoughts & Beliefs* card. Rosie, read the positive words that help you unlock!"

Rosie said haltingly, "I am competent . . . and will be able . . . to do this."

Ruff blubbered, "I c-can conquer m-my f-f-fears."

They smiled. "Keep going, Ruff! Read another one," Flo said.

"Others will be supportive," he replied, looking at Ebb and Flo. They smiled again.

"All right!" Ebb declared. "You're reframing negative beliefs into positive ones. That'll give you the power to find a way over to New World, no matter how desperate things might seem."

They all practically jumped out of their skins when a bolt of lightning struck across the river, cracking a mighty oak as easily as a squirrel cracks a walnut. When they looked again, they saw that the lightning had dislodged what appeared to be a thick rope from the tree. Hanging down, its loose end skipped across the water.

"A vine!" Rosie cried.

"There's your way across!" Ebb said as he reached out with the handle of his umbrella and snagged the vine.

"Over you go," said Ebb. "Up the vine and over."

"But what if it breaks? What if I fall?" wailed Ruff.

"Ruff!" Rosie said. "Reframe your thoughts—fast! How many thousands of vines have we climbed in our lives? That vine is thick enough to support Blink, for cryin' out loud!"

"But what about Ebb and Flo?"

"We'll meet you on the other side," Ebb said. "Don't you worry. We'll find another way."

"Then why don't we find it *with* you," Ruff pleaded. "Or we could go back to Blink's cave. I think we all should wait there for the storm to pass, don't you?"

"No," said Flo. "There's no reason to turn back now. Not anymore. Remember, you *can* be Change-Resilient!

"Go. Trust the vine. Trust yourself. And trust that we'll meet you on the other side!"

A large tree appeared, floating down the river, twisting and turning, its long branches grabbing everything in its path. "Look!" cried Ebb. "It's now or never. I won't be able to hold onto the vine when that tree comes through. Go now! Go!"

Rosie scampered onto the vine. "Are you coming with me, Ruff?" she shouted. "Please! I need you with me."

Then she turned and scampered along the vine into the smoldering oak, just as the twisting tree swept down the river, tearing the vine from Ebb's grasp.

"Ruff!" she cried, looking back across the river, seeing only Ebb and Flo.

"What?" Ruff said, grinning beside her in the tree.

From across Rushing River, Ebb and Flo called to their friends. "Remember—trust! Courage! And *Aim to Reframe!* We'll see you on the other side!"

CHAPTER ELEVEN

"My Behaviors"
Puzzle Piece

When dawn came the storm had passed. The morning found Rosie running in circles, searching frantically for Ebb and Flo. Ruff sat atop a tall hickory, working his Change Puzzle. Every so often he searched the forest floor for a glimpse of the couple.

That afternoon, after enjoying a lunch of raspberries Rosie had stumbled upon while searching for Ebb and Flo, Ruff spotted the duo making their way down the path toward his tall tree. The little squirrel was so happy to see them that he could barely chatter a signal to Rosie, who still raced chaotically through the underbrush.

The foursome greeted one another, and Ebb and Flo told their tale of being ferried across the river by a friendly forest ranger. "Now that we're all here in New World," Ebb said, "maybe we should get back to working the Change Puzzle so I can figure out how my behaviors are blocking me. I've gotta decide, one way or the other, in two days."

"Look," Ruff said smiling, as he held up his Change Puzzle, proudly displaying how he had connected four pieces together: *"It" Happens!*, *My Feelings*, *My Thoughts & Beliefs,* and *My Behaviors.*

Rosie looked at his puzzle and scratched her head. "How did you do that, Ruff? I can't fit this *My Behaviors* piece! No matter how hard I try. Even when I got here, my behaviors didn't seem to work. All I could do was run around in circles like a scared chipmunk."

Ebb laughed. "Don't worry. We'll teach you how to turn your good intentions into constructive action."

"Sometimes," said Flo, "a squirrel can lessen her anxiety just by keeping busy. But *busy* isn't always *productive*. The *My Behaviors* piece can help you learn the difference."

"What are my behaviors, anyway?" Rosie pondered.

"Behaviors are everything you say or do when you're affected by a change," said Ebb. "Changing behavior is very challenging! It's hard to change those things you say or do every day—your habits."

"Then why bother?" huffed Ruff, worried that perhaps he hadn't put his puzzle pieces together correctly after all.

"What if you could stop yourself from fretting all the time?" Ebb replied. "Would you bother to do that?"

Ruff's ears twitched with excitement. "Is that *possible?*"

Ebb laughed. "Yes, it is."

"And I can stop running around in circles without getting anything done?" cried Rosie.

"Sure," Flo said, as she reached in her backpack. "Here's a card that shows behaviors that lock and unlock us."

My Behaviors
Change Puzzle Card

These keep me **locked**	These help me **unlock**
· Reacting to the change haphazardly, without a plan	· Developing a plan broken down into achievable substeps
· Complaining about the change event	· Asking questions to better understand the change event
· Blaming others	· Acknowledging responsibility for making the change successful
· Becoming paralyzed or refusing to try new behaviors	· Learning more about the new behaviors needed; trying new behaviors
· Doing just enough to get by	· Going beyond what others expect
· Ridiculing others who change	· Encouraging others who change
· Talking behind others' backs or refusing to talk	· Talking directly with others
· Justifying my position	· Listening to others' positions
· Saying, "I HAVE to do this"	· Saying, "I CHOOSE to do this"
· Manipulating others into getting my Treasures	· Finding my own Treasures
· Fretting or talking about the bad things that will happen	· Talking about the positive things that could happen
· (Add my own)	· (Add my own)

Plan It Through, Then Do and Do

Ruff and Rosie studied the card. "Hmm," said Ruff, "I thought I had the puzzle piece for *My Behaviors* fitted just right. But now I see it's crooked.

"I see myself in that left-hand column of behaviors," Ruff continued. "I do fret too much. About owls. I fret about owls all the time. And that's me too," he pointed. "Doing just enough to get by."

"What about you, Rosie?" Flo asked. "Do you see any of the behaviors that keep you locked?"

"That first one—'Reacting to the change haphazardly, without a plan'—that's me in a nutshell," she replied. "To be honest, I'm the first to jump on a change, ready to go. I'm receptive to change, but I never seem to carry through."

"You know," Ebb said, "I've shared my feelings. And on the ferry ride over, Flo helped me reframe my thoughts and beliefs. But just like you, I'm worried I won't be able to change my behaviors to have the influence I want."

"So what behaviors are keeping you locked?" asked Flo.

"I've got to stop complaining about the new management team all the time," he replied, "and talking behind my boss's back. Sometimes I listen to myself and I can't believe it's me talking."

"Remember Sparky's advice," said Flo. "'Keep it simple. Pick a new behavior from the right-hand column, then try it at work.'"

Rosie was thinking deeply now. "Ebb, if you decided to stay with your job, which new behavior would you try first?"

Ebb looked thoughtfully at the card. "'Talking directly with others.' First thing I'd do is talk to my boss to find out what goals we have in common."

Flo added, "Don't forget to use the tip on the card, *Plan It Through, Then Do and Do.*"

"That's what Sparky taught me when I first started working for him," Ebb continued. "Because you know how hard it is with new things. In the beginning, you always feel awkward, artificial—"

"Like early in your career when you started making presentations to the design team," Flo said.

"Gosh, I was awful," Ebb laughed. "But I didn't give up. I used the tip, *Plan It Through, Then Do and Do.*"

"Ebb even rehearsed at home. And before too long new behaviors started to replace the old ones," said Flo.

"It helps to practice a new behavior at least a dozen times to make it a habit," Ebb added.

"So, where do I start?" asked Rosie. "I'm sick and tired of running in circles."

CHAPTER TWELVE

Ruff and Rosie Plan and Do—But Have Bad Luck

"First decide what Treasures you want to find here in New World," Flo suggested. "It's always easier to carry out a plan if you know what you value."

Ebb picked up two sticks and handed them to Ruff and Rosie. "Here—write the Treasures you want in the dust, right there."

So they wrote:

> Food—nuts, pinecones, berries
> Water
> Nice tree home
> Safety from snakes and owls
> Nice friends

"Good," Ebb said. "Now what actions must you take to get those things? What will your new behaviors need to be?"

Rosie said, "We need to make a plan—like it says on the card, broken down into achievable substeps."

"So how would you go about finding this tree home?" asked Ebb.

"Look for it, I guess," Rosie said.

"Run around again, go ahead," sniped Ruff. "Why don't we just find other squirrels and ask them?" He flicked his tail disdainfully. "'Cause they're gonna know New World a heck of a lot better than we do."

"That's a good idea. Let's look to the north first. If that doesn't work, we'll search the southern area," said Rosie.

"Good plan," Ruff said. "So go ahead, Rosie. Find some other squirrels and I'll stay here and help Ebb and Flo settle in."

"Hey!" Rosie exclaimed. "This is your idea, finding other squirrels. You're coming with me! We're supposed to be a team!"

"You know I'm no good at meeting new squirrels. You're more outgoing than I am."

"Well, maybe that's a new behavior you should learn," Rosie angrily replied. "I'm not gonna let you manipulate me into getting your Treasures for you. Let's go!"

Ruff realized he was backsliding into his old pattern of doing just enough to get by. "You're right," he said sheepishly. "I'll go."

So Ruff and Rosie set out to find a new home. They scampered over hill and dale until they came upon a narrow ravine, where a weasel was sullenly kicking the caps off a clump of toadstools.

Ruff stopped in his tracks when he noticed that one of the weasel's ears was chewed off.

"Hey!" the weasel challenged. "What're youse two doin' in my ravine? I'm Spike, and this is my turf!"

The hair rose on the back of Ruff's neck. He knew trouble when he saw it. But Rosie, for some bizarre reason, said, "Hi, I'm Rosie! And this is my friend, Ruff. We've just come to New World and we're looking for a place to live."

"You mean like in a tree or somethin'?" asked Spike.

Ruff's stomach became a knot. "Mom warned me about weasels!" he whispered to Rosie. "Let's run for it."

"Maybe we need to reframe our thinking about weasels too," she replied.

At that moment, Spike appeared beside Rosie. "You gotta meet Fester," he said, taking her arm. "He likes squirrels like you."

Suddenly, Ruff spotted a sharp silhouette perched on the limb of a gnarled tree. "Owl!" he screamed. "Run for it!"

Both squirrels rocketed away. They felt the owl's hot breath on their tails just as they careened into a hollow log. Gasping for air, they looked back to see the owl glaring at them. Luckily, the log was too narrow for the bird to enter.

However, in the distance, they heard Spike yelling, "Hold 'em, Fester, 'til I get there!" The weasel was running full tilt.

"Follow me," a voice whispered. And without thinking twice, the two squirrels chased a fluffy white tail down a rabbit hole at the base of the hollow log. They raced along a black corridor and didn't stop running until they reached the riverbank.

When they stumbled back into camp and told their story, Ebb and Flo shook their heads in dismay. "That's terrible!" they replied. "Awful!"

"New World is awful," said Ruff angrily. "Weasels and owls are teamed up. It stinks! Rosie and me are goin' back to Old World where we belong!"

"No!" exclaimed Flo. "Not tonight!"

"You guys have a good plan," Ebb said, "to find other squirrels who know the lay of the land—"

"What we found were predators!"

"Yes, you did," Flo sympathized. "Which created a bad *consequence.*"

"Everything you do or say has consequences," Ebb added. "That's what the next piece of the puzzle is about. But unfortunately, good behaviors sometimes have terrible consequences."

"That's the definition of bad luck," said Flo. "And as Sparky always says, 'Everything changes, including your luck.'"

"We were lucky to run into that rabbit or whoever it was," said Rosie.

"There you have it!" said Flo. "It seems your luck may have started to change already. But once you work the next piece of the puzzle you'll find that you won't have to rely on luck to be successful."

CHAPTER THIRTEEN

"Consequences to Me"
Puzzle Piece

The next day, as Ruff and Rosie discussed where they might meet a squirrel to help them find a new home, Ebb and Flo agreed that the squirrels needed to learn about *consequences*.

Just as Ruff and Rosie's "discussion" was about to disintegrate into an argument, Flo called out, "Be careful of the *consequences!*"

The squirrels stopped bickering. "Wha' do you mean?" said Ruff.

"I mean there might be negative consequences to your argument," Flo said.

Ebb picked up a stick and wrote in the dust in front of the two quizzical squirrels:

> Consequences
> are things that happen
> <u>after</u> my behavior,
> and either <u>encourage</u>
> or <u>discourage</u> it
> from happening again.

"Think about yesterday," he said. "You found a new raspberry patch, right? The berries were good. They were the consequence that encouraged you to go back there this morning for breakfast.

"But if the consequence to you is bad, like with the weasel and the owl, well, are you going back to that ravine today?"

"No way!" they exclaimed.

"Look, if I'm gonna stay at my job," Ebb continued, as he sat down beside them, "I'll have to encourage new, positive behaviors in myself and keep them going."

"How would you do that?" Rosie asked.

"Well, at work I'd associate with people who encourage me. I'd stick with people who help me carry the best from my old company into the new one. And I wouldn't give much weight to the opinions of people who discouraged me or tried to stop me. And I'd reinforce myself with positive self-talk."

"And I'd reinforce him too," added Flo. "All the time I'd keep telling him he's doing the right thing. Which you would be doing, dear."

"Dealing with change is easier if someone supports you," Ebb said, as he slipped his arm around Flo's shoulder.

Rosie smiled at Ruff. "Ruff and I are lucky to have each other too."

"When you're handling change, you might need help," Flo replied. "Especially if you lack self-discipline or you're stuck.

"Find someone to talk to. It could be a good friend. Or, it could even be someone professionally trained. The key is to find someone who will provide sound guidance and encouragement.

"Hey Ebb—when you were worried about moving from sales to design—remember that checklist we put on the refrigerator?" Flo smiled.

"We oughta do that again," Ebb replied. "That helped us track how many times we encouraged and discouraged each other!"

"Oh my!" Flo said. "As much as we were trying to help each other, a lot of the time we just created negative consequences by criticizing each other."

"But the checklist reminded us to be encouraging," Ebb said. Then he pulled another card from his jacket and handed it to Ruff and Rosie. "We have a card for consequences, of course."

"Of course," said Ruff, as the squirrels studied the card.

Consequences to Me
Change Puzzle Card

These keep me **locked**

- I experience negative outcomes for trying new behaviors (e.g., others discourage me; bad things happen)

- I get sympathy from others for old behaviors

- I can manipulate others into doing things because they feel sorry for me or want to avoid confronting me

- I provide negative feedback to myself (such as, "I just messed up and can't recover")

- I stay in my comfort zone

- I'm overwhelmed—the goal is too big and I punish myself for my paralysis

- (Add my own)

These help me **unlock**

- I experience positive outcomes for trying new behaviors (e.g., others encourage me; good things happen)

- I get encouragement from others for new behaviors

- I am proud of what I've been able to do for myself

- I provide encouraging feedback to myself (such as, "We all make mistakes, it's part of learning")

- I purposefully leave my comfort zone to gain confidence

- I set smaller goals and reward myself when I achieve them

- (Add my own)

Find Encouragement, Avoid Discouragement

"I see where we went wrong, Ruff. We were bickering again. Just now. That discouraged us. The weasel and owl were discouraging enough without us discouraging ourselves."

"A solution to discouraging consequences," declared Flo, "is to create *positive* ones. It's the most powerful way to change your behavior, to *create your own positive consequences!*"

"Flo's right," Ebb said, pointing to the tip on the bottom of the card: **Find Encouragement, Avoid Discouragement.**

"Sometimes you can't avoid negative consequences," he added. "Like yesterday with the weasel and the owl. But if you create more encouraging consequences, like the raspberries, then the occasional setbacks won't get you down!"

"Remember, it's your *feelings, thoughts,* and *beliefs* that help you get a new behavior started. But it's the *positive consequences* that keep a new behavior going. So don't rely on luck—create your own positive consequences!"

"Okay, Ruff," Rosie said. "From now on, we support each other. And we offer each other nothing but encouragement!"

CHAPTER FOURTEEN

Ruff and Rosie Try Again

"You two have a plan," said Ebb. "The question now is: Are you ready to try again to find new Treasures in New World?"

"Yes!" Ruff and Rosie declared. So they set out again to find a new tree home—but in the opposite direction this time. Ruff and Rosie hopped until they came upon a small clearing where four elderly squirrels played croquet with tiny mallets and acorns for balls.

"Excuse me. I'm Rosie, and this is my best friend Ruff. We're looking for a new home."

"And we were wondering," Ruff added, "if any hickory trees around here belonged to anybody."

"This is a retirement community, sonny," explained one squirrel. "Try Big Bear Ridge. It's over there," he pointed.

"Okay," Ruff said, a bit crestfallen.

As they scampered toward Big Bear Ridge, Rosie encouraged Ruff: "Don't get down—that was just our first try. There are plenty of hickories, I'm sure!"

On the ridge stood a lone oak, laden with acorns. "Oooh!" said Rosie. "Look. An oak is nice."

"I don't like it," groused Ruff. "I thought we were looking for a hickory."

"Don't be negative," Rosie chided.

"You're right. An oak *is* sturdier," he said positively.

But as they inspected the tree, Ruff sniffed the air, then turned and spotted an opening in some nearby rocks. "Smell that?"

"A fox," Rosie said. "Scratch the oak."

As they journeyed deeper and deeper into the unfamiliar forest, the squirrels grew anxious. "Rosie, I'm getting discouraged," Ruff admitted.

"Me too. But we must keep going until we find a place."

"I'm exhausted," Ruff protested. "Let's climb this tree and rest a bit. Please."

Rosie agreed but added, "We're gonna go on all night if we have to until we find a home."

So they climbed until they sat atop a tree that looked out over New World. And right before them were several squirrels, dining in a beautiful butternut tree, laden with plump nuts.

"Oh my," gasped Rosie. "What a location! Too bad it's fully occupied."

"Hey, you don't know that. Test your thinking," Ruff challenged. "That's a big tree—maybe there's room. Dare to ask!"

Rosie took a deep breath. "Hi! Any room in that tree for us?"

"It's full," said one of the squirrels curtly.

"Well, are any others available?"

"Right there," one pointed.

"Thanks," Rosie said. "We're new to the area."

Ruff and Rosie hopped to the tree, a tall butternut, and scrambled up into its canopy. High in the thick leafy cover was a perfect hole for their nest.

They looked at each other, cried "HOME!" and scurried back to Ebb and Flo, who were preparing dinner.

"We found it!" they shouted. "Our new home—in a super butternut tree!"

"Congratulations, you two—you did it!" cried Ebb and Flo. "Now let's look at the consequences of your behavior."

"Aw, gee. Can't we just enjoy the moment?" protested Ruff.

"Of course you can. But if you analyze it while the experience is fresh," Ebb replied, "your actions and their positive consequences will be clear, and you'll know what to do next time!"

"I'm ready," said Rosie.

"Me too, then," grumped Ruff.

"Your behavior was to seek a new home, and your consequence is that you found a beauty. Now, are there any other consequences?"

Rosie spoke first. "I'm proud of what I accomplished!"

And Ruff said, "Me too. I left my comfort zone and it paid off! Finally! And I feel more confident now too!"

Ebb beamed. "Now you see the positive consequences of persevering with your plan."

"We've watched your *feelings, thoughts, beliefs,* and *behaviors* become unlocked, and now you have the payoff: positive *consequences!*" said Flo.

As the friends dined that night, they marveled at the changes they had undergone over the past few days: becoming fast friends, finding a new home, and meeting new challenges using the Change Puzzle. Not even the screech of an owl could keep them from sleeping soundly that night.

CHAPTER FIFTEEN

"My Impact on Others"— The Final Piece

The next morning, Ebb and Flo helped Ruff and Rosie move into their new home. The squirrels gathered leaves and branches for their nest while Ebb laid a flagstone patio at the base of the butternut tree. Flo carved "Number 1 Butternut Grove" on the trunk to let everyone in the neighborhood know that new squirrels had moved in.

"You know, Ruff," said Rosie, as she laid a thick layer of dried moss at the bottom of the nest. "We have to do something special for Ebb and Flo before they leave for Sparky's."

Ruff looked down at the couple, working at the base of the tree. "We could cook *them* dinner," he said.

"Flo's berry pie will be too hard to top," Rosie fretted.

"Think positive thoughts," encouraged Ruff.

"I guess I could make butternut pasta with black currant sauce—"

"And I could make wild green salad—with all the Queen Anne's lace and dandelions growing around here!" he replied.

"You finish the nest," Rosie said. "I'm going to gather some black currants." And with that, she raced down the trunk of the butternut tree.

"Where are you goin'?" asked Ebb, as he set the last flagstone in place.

"Oh, nowhere!" sang Rosie cheerily as she disappeared into a bramble bush.

"Flo, we need to leave for Sparky's after we get these kids moved in," Ebb said. "I've gotta make a decision by tomorrow. Maybe we should just take Ruff and Rosie with us. That way they can get Change Keys of their own."

"Want yours back, do you?" said Flo.

Ebb laughed at himself. "I do feel a bit naked without it. Do you think that's what's blocking me?"

"No." She closed her pocketknife. "Help me clean up these wood chips and gather some flowers. I have a feeling we're gonna get a dinner invitation, and I'd like to bring something pretty as a house-warming gift."

After Ebb and Flo swept the patio, they headed toward a creek to pick daffodils.

"You've hardly talked about retiring at all," Flo said. "What do you think that means?"

"It means I need to talk to Sparky!"

When they had gone, Ruff sneaked out from behind the tree, carrying a bulging sack of butternuts. He set it down, and with a Herculean effort he lifted the flagstone Ebb had just laid.

Then the squirrel quickly dug a hole, tossed in the sack of butternuts, shoved the flagstone over his cache, and dusted his paws. "Mine. All mine," he said before he raced back up the tree to finish the nest.

That evening they all sat on the patio, enjoying Rosie's butternut pasta and Ruff's wild green salad.

"You'll be going on to Sparky's soon, I guess," said Rosie.

"Yes," Flo replied, "but there is one final piece to the Change Puzzle, *My Impact on Others,* that Ebb and I must discuss with you before we go. This last piece will help you become aware of how your behaviors affect others."

"If we were hermits," said Ebb, "we wouldn't even have to consider this piece. But we're social animals— not like a lone wolf, say, who lives all by himself."

"You're right. Squirrels are different from wolves," Ruff said, nonchalantly eyeing the flagstone hiding his butternut stash. He realized that he hadn't done a very good job of leveling the stone, which seesawed every time somebody walked on it.

"Believe it or not," continued Flo, "It's possible to fit all your other puzzle pieces together yet still have a negative effect on others. So the trick is to discover if your behaviors are having a positive or negative effect."

"Okay . . . ?" said Ruff.

"For example," Ebb replied, "My new boss at work— he exercises all the time—at least two hours every evening after work. The *consequences to himself* are wonderful—he looks like a million bucks and I bet he feels great too."

"However," added Flo, "he doesn't realize the negative impact his behavior is having on his family."

"He's never home," said Ebb.

"His wife is very lonely," said Flo. "And the children cry for their father all the time."

"Of course, this isn't what the guy wants at all!" Ebb said. "When you listen to him talk, you know he loves his wife and kids."

"Why's he doing it then?" asked Ruff.

"It's complicated," said Ebb. "He's in his 40s, he isn't getting any younger. Personally, I think his intentions are good. He wants to look good for his wife and stay healthy for the kids—"

"But the point is," said Flo, "no matter what your motives are, you need to be aware of the impact your behavior has on other people. Especially people you really care about."

"How do I do that?" asked Ruff.

"Ask them!" said Ebb as he reached into his knapsack. "And here's a card we use to help us figure out whether our behavior is having a positive or negative impact on someone—"

Rosie stood up. "Why don't you let Ruff and me write up our own card for *Impact on Others?*" she said. "Without any help."

"Sure!" Ebb said. "Go for it! Sparky gave us some blank cards for just these occasions. The more you use the puzzle, the more you'll want to develop your own tip sheets."

Flo produced a blank card from her backpack. The two squirrels huddled on the far side of the patio as Ebb and Flo busied themselves clearing the dinner plates and brewing more tea. They watched as Ruff and Rosie wrote and scratched and scribbled and amended until they waved their card triumphantly. "We're done!" they exclaimed. And they read their card to Ebb and Flo.

My Impact on Others

Change Puzzle Card

My **Negative** Impact on Others	My **Positive** Impact on Others
· Others are embarrassed by my actions	· Others are proud of me
· Others worry about me	· Others know I'll be fine
· Others distrust me	· Others trust me
· Others avoid me	· Others seek me out
· Others are hurt by me	· Others feel supported by me
· Others clam up around me or edit what they say	· Others freely share their thoughts with me
· Others make excuses for me	· Others don't need to make excuses for me because I take responsibility for my own actions
· Others do my work for me (they enable me to continue my ineffective old behaviors)	· Others can count on me to carry my fair share of the work
· Others dislike me	· Others like me or respect me
· (Add my own)	· (Add my own)

Check My Effect

"Excellent work!" Ebb said as he crossed the patio to hand them each another cup of tea. "Those are great examples of the impact your behaviors can have on others!"

Suddenly Ebb stopped. "I didn't do a very good job of setting this stone, did I?"

But as Ebb bent over to take a closer look, Ruff jumped to his feet. "Don't worry about that now, Ebb! I'll take care of it in the morning!"

"No, no," Ebb replied as he lifted the stone. "When I do a job, I like to do it right. Hey!" he exclaimed. "There's a sack of butternuts under here!"

Rosie looked at the cache of nuts. "Those weren't there this morning, were they?" she asked. Then she turned to Ruff.

"I was just making sure I'd have enough nuts—I mean *we'd* have enough—just in case, or if by chance—"

"Ruff!" cried Rosie. "After all we've been through together, and you hide nuts from me? *Didn't you consider the impact your behavior would have on me, Ruff? Gee!*"

Ruff hung his head. "I'm sorry, Rosie."

Exasperated, Rosie marched over with the card and took Ruff by the arm. "We need to talk," she said. When she had dragged Ruff behind the butternut tree, she whispered, "This is embarrassing! You hide nuts for yourself, and I've got to find out in front of our guests?" She held the card up for Ruff to see. "Read number one for me, please."

He read it quietly, ashamedly. "I'll work to make you proud of me." Then a tear rolled down his face. Then another and another and another as he thought about how foolish, negative, and self-absorbed he'd been ever since the fire.

"I'm sorry, Rosie," he sniffled. "You're my best friend. I would never want to do anything to hurt your feelings or to embarrass you! I promise to use the tip we wrote at the bottom of the card, every day! To remind me to *Check My Effect.* I promise!"

Then Rosie hugged him. "You've come a long way, Ruff."

"We both have, Rosie."

CHAPTER SIXTEEN

The Power Is Within You

The next morning Ruff and Rosie watched as Ebb and Flo packed their backpacks, preparing to hurry on to Sparky's. For some reason, Ruff was unusually nervous, racing back and forth, trying to help them pack, but somehow always foiling their efforts to get the job done.

Meanwhile Ebb was wracking his brain, trying to figure if there was anything he and Flo had forgotten to tell their friends about handling change.

"Oh yeah. Remember—the Change Puzzle can help turn a crisis into an opportunity," Ebb said.

"We know that, Ebb," Rosie replied.

"Yeah, that's right. You do. Here," he said. "This last little card summarizes the Change Puzzle tips." He handed the card to Rosie.

Change Puzzle Tips

My Feelings	**Become Aware, Then Share**
My Thoughts & Beliefs	**Aim to Reframe**
My Behaviors	**Plan It Through, Then Do and Do**
Consequences to Me	**Find Encouragement, Avoid Discouragement**
My Impact on Others	**Check My Effect**

"Ebb," Flo said, "if we stick around much longer, you won't have to decide whether or not to retire. They'll fire you for gross absenteeism!"

"I guess we better go, huh," Ebb said reluctantly.

"We're very proud of you two," said Flo. "You've both learned so much."

"But we're never done!" Ruff said. "I know that. I know I can't get complacent and slip back into negativity and self-doubt, but—"

"Keep working your Change Puzzle each time *it happens*. It only works if you work it," said Ebb.

"How can we ever thank you?" Rosie asked.

"Just pass the message on to your friends and to everyone you meet—pay it forward," said Flo. "Now, we need to be on our way."

"Oh, here, Ebb. I almost forgot. I wanted to give this back," Ruff said as held out his paw. In it glowed Ebb's golden Change Key.

Ebb reached out for his key but stopped himself. "No, no, you keep it."

"I couldn't," replied Ruff. "Yesterday, when I was waiting to bury that stupid bag of nuts, I heard you and Flo talking."

"I don't think I need that key anymore, Ruff," Ebb said.

"But I've used it. I know how powerful its magic can be," the squirrel replied.

"Let me explain something," Ebb said. "I've thought about the key since Flo and I talked.

"In the past, I relied on that key to help me handle change. I thought I needed the key to make the words on the back come true."

Ruff flipped the key over to reveal the words, **UNLOCK YOURSELF!**

Ebb continued, "But I've learned a few things since I met you and Rosie. And one thing I learned is that the key's power really comes from inside." Ebb pointed to his heart.

"Inside you?" Ruff asked.

"And inside you," Ebb replied, touching the squirrel's tiny chest.

"And I've also learned," he said as he looked at his wife, "that Flo and I used the puzzle to *react* to change. But now I know that I have the power inside me to be Change-Resilient all the time. I can use the Change Puzzle to handle things proactively."

"Even before change happens?" asked Flo.

"Yep. That way maybe I can create the kind of company I want to work for—I can create the change," Ebb said with a grin.

"But I know how much this key means to you!" Ruff persisted.

"I should've seen this merger coming," Ebb said regretfully. "But if I know Sparky, he's gonna have a tip or two on how to use the puzzle to get ahead of the game—not only to make the company what I want it to be, but to handle some other big changes before they happen too."

"Like when we finally do retire?" asked Flo.

Ebb nodded.

"But—" Ruff protested.

"No," Ebb said. "That key's yours."

"And this one's yours," said Flo, draping her golden key around Rosie's neck. "You've earned it."

Suddenly Ruff started shaking. The little squirrel shook so much that he had to use Ebb's Change Key, like a cane, to steady himself.

"What in the world's come over you?" asked Flo. "Are you ill?"

"Don't go," he said. "Please don't go!"

"But we've got to," Flo said, trying to comfort him.

"It's all moving too fast. We just got to New World! We just settled into our new home. I don't want you to go! I'm not ready yet! I need more time!"

"Ruff," Rosie said gently. "Get your Change Puzzle out. Check your feelings and your thoughts and beliefs—"

"All right, all right," Ruff said.

"You can puzzle through this situation," Ebb said. "And Rosie can help you."

CHAPTER SEVENTEEN

Ruff Becomes Change-Resilient!

"Okay, Ruff," said Flo, "work the Change Puzzle! What is your *"It" Happens?*"

"*It* hasn't happened yet. But it will. It'll happen the moment you and Ebb leave!"

"Okay," Ebb said. "Now, consider your feelings about our leaving. What feelings are keeping you locked so you're afraid to say good-bye? And what feelings will help unlock you?"

Ruff searched for the right word to describe his feelings. Rosie held out the *My Feelings* card, and he pointed a trembling paw at the ones that were his: sad, helpless, anxious, worried.

"And I'm afraid that I won't be able to use the Change Puzzle without you," he wailed.

Flo was about to speak when Rosie held up her paw. "Okay, Ruff," Rosie said. "And the feelings that can unlock you?"

"My feelings that can unlock me are excitement at the prospect of being independent in New World. And uhm . . . curiosity about this beautiful place. And happiness, because I'm with you, Rosie, and we're learning to support each other."

"Excellent!" Rosie said. "Now, what about your thoughts and beliefs?"

"Well, I guess I'm locked in my old thoughts, that my only Treasures are the friends I have right now. And I won't find any new ones tomorrow. And my belief is that we can't do this without Ebb and Flo.

"However, I am starting to believe that there are more hidden Treasures out there than I ever imagined. And I also think that Rosie and I will get better and better at working the puzzle!"

"Those are the thoughts and beliefs that will unlock you!" Rosie said. "Now, what about your behaviors? Start with the ones that are locking you."

"Well, I'm locked in my old behavior of not trying new behaviors. I've always been that way. But what would unlock me," he said, "is to try new behaviors in small, doable steps."

"That's a great idea for me too," Rosie replied.

"I guess I could start by saying good-bye to Ebb and Flo," Ruff added. "And then we could look for new friends once Ebb and Flo have left for Sparky's."

"And," continued Rosie, "what about your *Consequences to Me* puzzle piece?"

"Oh, boy! What are the consequences of my old behaviors to me? I'm comfortable with them, that's for sure—they make me feel secure. And I'm trying to control you and Ebb and Flo to stay here and take away my worries.

"And, Rosie, I'm sorry about that. I am. I'll try to change. But I'll need you to be patient with me and to encourage me, even if I'm just taking baby steps."

"I promise."

"But don't do things for me that I can do for myself," Ruff added. "You do that all the time. I need to learn to rely on myself for once."

Rosie smiled. "Consider it done."

Ruff beamed. "And finally, what is my behavior's impact on others? Golly, I never intended to hurt you, Rosie. I didn't. I know I've embarrassed you and caused you a lot of worry and pain. I'm sorry."

"Apology accepted."

"The *impact* of my new behaviors will be . . . hopefully others will find me to be a lot more fun, more interesting, and a heck of a lot easier to live with!"

"Great, Ruff!" cried Rosie. "You have broken through at last!"

"Ebb! Flo!" Ruff cried. "This is wonderful! You've just seen a squirrel unlock right before your very eyes! Ebb? Flo?"

"Where did they go?" whispered Rosie.

The couple had vanished. Ruff and Rosie scampered to the top of their tree but couldn't see far down the path for all the foliage that surrounded their beautiful new home.

"They must've gone when we were working the Change Puzzle," said Rosie.

"All by ourselves," said Ruff. He held out his paw and Rosie slapped a smooth low-five.

There they were, alone together in New World for the very first time.

"Come on," Ruff said.

"Where?" asked Rosie.

"Follow me."

Epilogue

"Where are you taking me?" called Rosie. She chased after Ruff, who ran down the path, veered off to leap a small stream, and scampered up a high hill to a wide ridge that overlooked a large expanse of New World.

"Have we been here before?" asked Rosie.

"This is Big Bear Ridge, remember?" said Ruff. "Come on!" he exclaimed, and they scampered up the trunk of an evergreen tree.

Far in the distance, the two squirrels spied Ebb and Flo making their way along the forest path. The couple walked hand in hand. Ruff and Rosie could see, even from a mile away, that their friends were chatting contentedly. They watched silently until Ebb and Flo disappeared at a bend in the path.

Suddenly they were shocked from their reverie by a terrible shaking. The evergreen bucked and swayed as if buffeted by an angry wind. Looking down, they saw a great bear scratching his wide behind on the trunk of the tree.

"Blink!" they yelled.

But the bear was oblivious to them. Having satisfied his itch, he lumbered along the ridge to a honey tree and immediately climbed it. He reached into an opening in the tree with his gigantic paw and pulled out a piece of the comb, dripping with honey.

Bees swarmed out of their hive and angrily attacked Blink, buzzing and stinging to drive the bear from their home.

Watching from a safe distance, Ruff and Rosie could see that Blink looked quite content to gulp down the honey as the bees danced in a frenzy around him.

"Hey, Blink!" they shouted again.

Blink turned his great face toward them, smeared with honey and angry bees.

"Hey! Ruff and Rosie! Want some?" He offered them a piece of the honeycomb crawling with angry insects.

Ruff and Rosie looked at each other. "No thanks."

"Mighty good," he said, his lips starting to swell from the bee stings.

"You appear to be doing well," they called.

"Oh yeah," he replied. "You know me! 'Go with your gut,' that's what I always say!"

Rosie turned to Ruff and asked quietly, "Do you think we should pass on the message of the Change Puzzle to Blink?" She turned the puzzle over in her paws.

"We could, but I don't think Blink needs it. I think he's one of those rare creatures whose puzzle pieces fall into place naturally."

"Instinctively," Rosie replied.

"Yeah. He works his puzzle in the moment, without thinking."

"Do you think that's a good thing or a bad thing?" Rosie wondered.

"It seems to work for him," Ruff said. "When the fire happened, he didn't fool himself by pretending everything was okay. He adapted and now seems happy. He's not interested in analyzing things."

"The only thing he's interested in," Rosie replied, "is what's right in front of him—"

"Honey," Ruff and Rosie said in unison.

"But, Ruff," Rosie said, "I'm interested in much more than that."

"Me too," Ruff replied as he touched his Change Key.

Then the two squirrels bade Blink farewell and hopped back to Number 1 Butternut Grove, where they climbed to their nest and happily regarded what they had created.

Through their struggle to accept change, they had found their hidden Treasures. *And the greatest Treasure of all was learning how to become* **Change-Resilient.**

The End

Pulling "It" All Together

"Readers of ***"It" Happens!*** asked me to pull together all of the change tools into one spot so they could immediately begin to work through change in their lives. I hope the following guide is helpful to you on your journey through life's changes."

—JULIE SMITH

This guide will help you pull together all of the pieces of the Change Puzzle presented in *"It" Happens!* Use this guide to work through any change that is affecting you currently.

The goal is to become Change-Resilient.

> Change-Resilient—to adjust easily, with courage and confidence, when "it" (a change) happens

When you become Change-Resilient, you'll be able to:

- Handle any change, even a crisis
- Move forward—get past fear, unlock, and open yourself to opportunities
- Find the Treasures that are always hidden or unexpected in every change
- Improve the overall quality of your life

> Treasures—the things you value, from material things to intangibles such as relationships, respect from others, time for yourself, and so on. Most people fear change because they are afraid of losing their Treasures.

You become Change-Resilient by working each piece of the Change Puzzle and putting the pieces together in a way you can be proud of. The pieces of the puzzle are described on the next page.

The Change Puzzle Pieces

1. **"It" Happens!** is any change that affects me. It can be expected or unexpected, welcome or unwelcome, planned or unplanned, under my control or out of it, caused by nature or by people.

2. **My Feelings** are the emotions I experience when going through a change.

3. **My Thoughts & Beliefs**—thoughts are ideas that run through my head about the change. They are private and known only to me. Beliefs are opinions that I hold deep inside as absolute truths.

4. **My Behaviors** are everything I say or do when I am affected by a change.

5. **Consequences to Me** are things that occur after my behaviors and either encourage or discourage me from doing the same behaviors again.

6. **My Impact on Others** is about the effect my behaviors have on others.

Always start with the piece named **"It" Happens!**
"It" is any change that affects you. It's the trigger
for working your Change Puzzle.

Description of my "It"

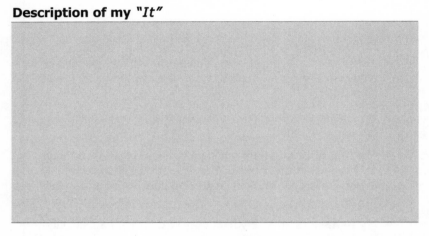

The next step is to assess your level of Change-Resilience. Use the
change-resilience meter shown on the next page to determine
whether you are:

- **Resisting the change**—like Ruff in the story,
  "It" Happens!, you might be locked up by your negative
  feelings, thoughts, and beliefs about the change. You
  might be unwilling to move forward until you understand
  what possible good could come from the change.

- **Receptive to the change**—like Rosie, you might be
  emotionally ready for the change and believe that it will
  result in good things. However, you are not yet Change-
  Resilient because you are struggling to turn your good
  thoughts and intentions into positive action.

- **Resilient**—you are like Ebb and Flo, able to adjust easily to
  the change by working the pieces of the Change Puzzle in-
  the-moment as the change unfolds.

My Change-Resilience Meter

	Yes	No	Unsure
1. Am I proud of how I'm handling this **"It"?**	☐	☐	☐
2. Are **My Feelings** about the change positive?	☐	☐	☐
3. Are **My Thoughts & Beliefs** about the change positive?	☐	☐	☐
4. Am I proud of **My Behaviors?** · Am I doing things I feel good about? · Am I doing things I believe in? · Am I doing things that help me move forward?	☐	☐	☐
5. Are the **Consequences to Me** encouraging my positive behaviors?	☐	☐	☐
6. Is **My Impact on Others** positive, especially people I care about?	☐	☐	☐

No to questions 2 or 3

Yes to 2 & 3; No to 1, 4, 5, or 6

Yes to all questions

I'M RESISTANT   **I'M RECEPTIVE**   **I'M RESILIENT**

If I checked "no" or "unsure" to any question, I should continue to work the Change Puzzle pieces until I can honestly answer "yes."

My Feelings

Feelings are the emotions you experience when you are going through a change. Feelings exist for a reason: they help you know what to do when faced with a change. For example, your feelings might warn you to flee from real dangers, caution you to move slowly, or tell you when you're on the right track.

Use this Change Puzzle Card to check your feelings. On the left are feelings that signal you are locked and resisting the change. On the right are feelings that signal you are unlocked and receptive to the change. The goal is to move toward feelings that unlock you. The tip at the bottom of the card tells you how to begin to unlock your feelings.

Another way to unlock your feelings is to work the next piece of the puzzle—negative thoughts and beliefs can cause feelings that keep you locked.

My Feelings
Change Puzzle Card

These keep me **locked**	These help me **unlock**
· Fearful	· Courageous and confident
· Resentful	· Appreciative, accepting
· Angry	· Calm, determined
· Sad	· Happy, joyful
· Guilty, embarrassed, ashamed	· Proud, worthy
· Depressed, lethargic	· Excited, energetic
· Helpless, powerless	· Confident, capable, powerful
· Ambivalent, confused	· Committed, focused
· Trapped	· Liberated
· Anxious, worried	· Relaxed
· Hopeless	· Hopeful
· Judgmental	· Empathetic
· Apathetic	· Curious
· (Add my own)	· (Add my own)

Become Aware, Then Share

One sign that you are becoming Change-Resilient is that your feelings will become more unlocked as the change unfolds. Use the Change Puzzle Card to identify and track your feelings over time to see how you are progressing.

My Current Feelings	Date	Actions I Will Take to Further Unlock My Feelings*

*Possible Actions to Unlock My Feelings

Become Aware, Then Share—Identify my feelings and find a safe place to discuss them. This will help me let go of feelings that are keeping me locked.

☐ Listen to my body and record the signals it is giving me directly about how I'm feeling. (If my stomach tightens, I might be nervous. If my heart races, I might be excited)

☐ Ask others to provide me with feedback on my body language if I can't pick up the the direct signals my body is sending. (Sometimes emotions show up indirectly though tone of voice, facial expressions, and other forms of body language)

☐ Use the Change Puzzle Card to name my feelings

☐ Use my locked feelings (such as anger) to spur me to positive action and not get stuck in negativity

☐ Develop an understanding of what I fear most about the change

☐ Share my feelings with a trusted confidante who will listen, be nonjudgmental, and help me move forward

Thoughts are ideas that run through your head and help you make sense of things when *it happens.* Beliefs are opinions that you hold deep inside as absolute truths. To become Change-Resilient, you have to be willing to challenge your own thoughts and beliefs, to see whether they are still useful to you in the new situation.

Use this Change Puzzle Card to identify your thoughts and beliefs that are keeping you locked and helping you unlock.

As you unlock your thoughts and beliefs, notice how your feelings change—they should be unlocking too.

My Thoughts & Beliefs
Change Puzzle Card

These keep me **locked**	These help me **unlock**
· I don't believe that anything positive will come from this	· I have faith that positive things will result from this
· I'll never be able to do this	· I am competent and will be able to do this
· My fears will conquer me	· I can handle this in spite of my fears. I can conquer my fears
· I am stuck here	· I have endless choices
· No one will help me	· Others will be supportive
· I don't deserve good things	· I deserve good things
· I can't count on myself to carry through	· I can accomplish what I set out to do
· Bad things will happen	· Good things will happen
· I will never be able to replace my Treasures	· I'll be able to find the hidden Treasures that are not yet apparent
· (Add my own)	· (Add my own)

Aim to Reframe
(Think positive thoughts; test my negative thoughts)

Use the Change Puzzle Card to identify and track your thoughts and beliefs as the change unfolds. It can be rewarding to track your progress.

My Current Thoughts & Beliefs	Date	Actions I Will Take to Further Unlock My Thoughts & Beliefs*

*Possible Actions to Unlock My Thoughts & Beliefs

Aim to Reframe—convert my negative thoughts into positive ones.

☐ Think positive thoughts—catch myself thinking a negative thought and immediately switch to a positive thought until "positive self-talk" becomes a habit. Track the number of times I catch myself thinking negatively each day, until I reduce that number significantly

☐ Test my negative thoughts—either jump into the situation to see if it's as bad as I thought or talk with others who think and act differently than I do to see what they think and believe about the change (this includes connecting with others personally or through their writings)

Behaviors are the things you say and do when affected by a change. It's important to align your behaviors with the two pieces of the puzzle that you worked earlier:

- My Feelings—Make sure you feel good about the things you say and do

- My Thoughts & Beliefs— Make sure you are not thinking one thing and doing another publicly (e.g., you smile publicly but think privately, "This is not right!")

My Behaviors
Change Puzzle Card

These keep me **locked**	These help me **unlock**
· Reacting to the change haphazardly, without a plan	· Developing a plan broken down into achievable substeps
· Complaining about the change event	· Asking questions to better understand the change event
· Blaming others	· Acknowledging responsibility for making the change successful
· Becoming paralyzed or refusing to try new behaviors	· Learning more about the new behaviors needed; trying new behaviors
· Doing just enough to get by	· Going beyond what others expect
· Ridiculing others who change	· Encouraging others who change
· Talking behind others' backs or refusing to talk	· Talking directly with others
· Justifying my position	· Listening to others' positions
· Saying, "I HAVE to do this"	· Saying, "I CHOOSE to do this"
· Manipulating others into getting my Treasures	· Finding my own Treasures
· Fretting or talking about the bad things that will happen	· Talking about the positive things that could happen
· (Add my own)	· (Add my own)

Plan It Through, Then Do and Do

Use the Change Puzzle Card to track your behaviors over time to see how you are progressing.

My Current Behaviors	Date	Actions I Will Take to Further Unlock My Behaviors*

*Possible Actions to Unlock My Behaviors

Plan It Through, Then Do and Do—decide which Treasures I want, then identify the behaviors that will help me find them. Then do and do these behaviors until they become a habit.

☐ Stop myself when I'm engaging in the behaviors that keep me locked. (Publicly call myself on it and commit to the "remedy" by saying something like, "There I go, I'm doing it again. I've slipped back into complaining about others behind their backs. Let's go talk to Jerry directly.")

☐ Select one behavior that will help unlock me and try it at least a dozen times until I become more comfortable doing it

☐ Get help from a friend or a professional if I'm not very self-disciplined in changing my behaviors or am unsure of what to do

Consequences are the things that happen after your behavior and either encourage or discourage it from happening again. During a change, positive behaviors can sometimes be followed by bad consequences. That's the definition of bad luck. Without encouraging consequences, you'll be tempted to give up and go back to doing what you've always done before the change. Work this piece of the puzzle to create your own encouraging consequences, so you won't have to rely on luck to keep making progress.

Consequences to Me
Change Puzzle Card

These keep me **locked**	These help me **unlock**
· I experience negative outcomes for trying new behaviors (e.g., others discourage me; bad things happen)	· I experience positive outcomes for trying new behaviors (e.g., others encourage me; good things happen)
· I get sympathy from others for old behaviors	· I get encouragement from others for new behaviors
· I can manipulate others into doing things because they feel sorry for me or want to avoid confronting me	· I am proud of what I've been able to do for myself
· I provide negative feedback to myself (such as, "I just messed up and can't recover")	· I provide encouraging feedback to myself (such as, "We all make mistakes, it's part of learning")
· I stay in my comfort zone	· I purposefully leave my comfort zone to gain confidence
· I'm overwhelmed—the goal is too big and I punish myself for my paralysis	· I set smaller goals and reward myself when I achieve them
· (Add my own)	· (Add my own)

Find Encouragement,
Avoid Discouragement

Do you want to change your behaviors? If so, as you work through the change, ensure that you are getting at least four *encouraging* consequences for your positive behaviors for every one *discouraging* consequence. Track these consequences below and make changes as needed.

Consequences to Me	Date	Actions I Will Take to Create More Encouraging Consequences*

*Possible Actions for Creating More Encouraging Consequences

Find Encouragement, Avoid Discouragement

☐ Ask others to provide me with feedback, especially encouraging feedback

☐ Provide myself with positive feedback

☐ Be aware of how I'm feeling after I've said or done something (feelings can be consequences too)

☐ Associate with people who offer encouragement

☐ Disregard feedback from others that is harmful or unnecessarily discouraging

☐ Take note of things when they go well

☐ Treat myself to something nice after I accomplish a goal

Unless you are a hermit, your behaviors during a change will have an impact on many others, from friends to family to co-workers to strangers. Work this piece of the puzzle to gain a deeper understanding of how your behaviors are affecting others you care about. Check to see that your actual effect on others matches what you intended.

My Impact on Others

Change Puzzle Card

My **Negative** Impact on Others	My **Positive** Impact on Others
· Others are embarrassed by my actions	· Others are proud of me
· Others worry about me	· Others know I'll be fine
· Others distrust me	· Others trust me
· Others avoid me	· Others seek me out
· Others are hurt by me	· Others feel supported by me
· Others clam up around me or edit what they say	· Others freely share their thoughts with me
· Others make excuses for me	· Others don't need to make excuses for me because I take responsibility for my own actions
· Others do my work for me (they enable me to continue my ineffective old behaviors)	· Others can count on me to carry my fair share of the work
· Others dislike me	· Others like me or respect me
· (Add my own)	· (Add my own)

Check My Effect

Use the Change Puzzle Card to track the impact you are having on others as the change unfolds. Take action as needed.

My Effect on People I Care About	Date	Actions I Will Take to Check My Effect*

*Possible Actions for Checking My Effect

☐ Ask others to tell me how my behaviors affect them

☐ When I do or say something, watch the body language of others to see how they are reacting to my behaviors. Check my interpretations of their body language with them to confirm my perceptions

☐ Thank others for providing me with feedback

☐ Be non-defensive in receiving the feedback and ask for further clarity, if needed

More Treasures

You have just discovered powerful keys to becoming Change-Resilient in today's fast-paced and ever-changing world. What's next? At LifePath, we're constantly creating nifty tools and creative ways to help you learn how to adapt and become Change-Resilient! Here are some of the ways LifePath can help you and your organization adapt to change—

"It" Happens™ WORKBOOK

Don't go through any change without a plan! LifePath's *"It" Happens Workbook* is an engaging way to problem-solve how you are *currently* handling the change versus how you would *like* to handle it.

Filled with fun facts and quotes, the workbook helps you through each step of the puzzle. You'll develop a comprehensive plan of action for handling the change. And you'll have room to journal and record how you're doing, so you can adjust your plan as the change unfolds.

CHANGE PUZZLE™ & CHANGE PUZZLE CARDS™

Keep these wonderful change tools on your desk, in your car, at home—or wherever change might hit you. Give copies to your friends and family to help them remember to put together the puzzle pieces in a way they can be proud of.

CHANGE-RESILIENCE SURVEY™

Use this self-scoring instrument to determine whether you are resistant, receptive, or resilient toward change. The assessment results include tips on how to become unlocked and open to new opportunities.

BE CHANGE-RESILIENT™ WORKSHOPS

In a two-hour session, all attendees will grasp how to use the Change Puzzle™ and Change Puzzle Cards™ to become Change-Resilient. A four-hour session shows leaders how to help others adjust easily with courage and confidence when *it happens* in their organizations.

BE CHANGE-RESILIENT™ PRESENTATION

Author Julie M. Smith brings these concepts to life through a 30- to 60-minute talk filled with wonderful stories and examples, weaving in changes that are specific to your organization or team.

To learn more about LifePath's products and services, visit our Website at:

www.lifepathonline.com

Acknowledgements

A short little book like this always looks like it could have been written in a weekend. In truth, the concepts in this book took me almost 25 years to pull together. And I am deeply grateful to the people who helped me along the way—

My Intellectual Guides. I usually learn things first by reading and researching. I like to know whether a promising tip is backed up by data. My parents, Dr. Gordon W. Smith and Isabelle M. Smith, started me down this path by creating an intellectually stimulating home environment. Later, Dr. Kennon A. Lattal, my doctoral advisor at West Virginia University, nurtured my desire to learn everything I could about the science of Behavior Analysis. In my early days of consulting, Dr. Jack Byrd encouraged me to extend my readings far and wide, to integrate learnings from a variety of disciplines into simple models that could be understood and used by all levels of employees.

My Colleagues and Clients. Once I've acquired the "head" knowledge, the next challenge I love is to apply it and see if it really works. I am forever indebted to my behavioral "soul sister," Dr. Leslie A. Braksick, for being courageous enough to cofound and lead CLG with me.

Leslie and other CLG consultants have repeatedly pushed the envelope in merging tools that bring about individual behavior change with those that engender large-scale, organization-wide change.

Together with our clients, we have pioneered some of the most effective behavior-based change tools available. It is because of my colleagues at CLG and our clients that I can say without reservation that the tools in this book work—they will embolden individuals to enact change both personally and professionally.

My Spiritual Mentors. It took me awhile to learn that head knowledge needs to translate into actions from the heart. Some of my colleagues helped me connect my head and heart simply by caring enough to provide feedback to me. To all of you, I am forever grateful.

My sister, Christine Miller, has always provided a ready ear and introduced me to many of the concepts in this book, especially those related to unlocking feelings and thoughts and beliefs. Thank you, Chris, for helping me take to heart a core life concept—that we really do determine the quality of our own lives, regardless of what happens to us.

My Book Team. It takes a village to create a book, especially one that blends a story line with rich content. My fellow villagers who fostered the development of this book are Fred Schroyer (chief editor and astute skeptic), Scott Frank (dialogue artist), Lisa Smith (most patient production manager), Dave Varner (chief supporter and office manager for LifePath), Blair Campbell (graphic designer), Tim Voigts (dust jacket designer), Michael Arnold (illustrator), Mary Jo Sontagg (concept developer), Roxanne Koepsell (best friend and marketing expert), Anne Palmer (book publishing consultant par excellence), Kathleen Hurson (product developer), and 60 reviewers who provided feedback that helped shape the story and change concepts. The encouraging words of all of the reviewers heartened me and helped me see that the book was worthy of a broader audience.

My Family. My husband Mickey was custom-made for me. I could not have found a more supportive spouse. Thank you, Mickey, for graciously welcoming editors and writers into our home and on our vacations. Your ability to adapt in the moment and live life to the fullest has been an inspiration for me and others who love you. Along with Jenny and Michael, you have made my life rich with animals, friends, and just plain fun.

About the Author

Dr. Julie Smith is passionate about simplifying complex concepts of human behavior so individuals and organizations can achieve unprecedented success.

Julie is cofounder and senior partner of CLG, a global consulting company that helps organizations implement strategies, manage change, and improve results through the consistent application of the science of human behavior. Her clients include major international organizations such as ChevronTexaco, Bayer Corporation, United Airlines, JPMorgan Chase, and others.

Regarded as a thought-leader in the field of performance improvement, Dr. Smith has devoted the past 20 years to helping companies achieve significant results in such diverse areas as leadership development, operational excellence, customer service, capital expenditures, and more.

Her extensive work with Fortune 100 companies led to the formation of a highly successful model for leading organization-wide change, as well as accompanying tools to help people understand *how* to enact change in global companies.

In response to growing demand for more specific behavioral information and tools to help individuals cope with change, Dr. Smith authored *"It" Happens! How to Become Change-Resilient* to provide a simple but profound breakthrough process for adapting to any change.

Dr. Smith also launched a new company called LifePath, an innovative provider of powerful personal change tools to help individuals adapt to change with courage and self-confidence.

Change is a constant theme in Julie's personal life too. Her husband, Mickey, and two stepchildren, Jenny and Michael, enrich the family's riverside park with a continual infusion of new animals and friends. Julie's beloved Welsh Corgi, Shorty, is the only unchanging presence in her life, always ready with a welcome smile and an open invitation to lay in the hammock.

Sharing *"It" Happens!* With Others

Now that you have learned how to become Change-Resilient, you can help others become Change-Resilient, too, by ordering additional copies of *"It" Happens!* today. Just call:

1-800-CEO-READ
(1-800-236-7323)

Julie M. Smith, Ph.D.

A Proven Way To Handle Change

"It" Happens!

How to Become Change-Resilient

"It" Happens! is also available through www.amazon.com or at your local bookstore.

For Volume Purchases

Generous quantity discounts are available for purchases of 50 books or more. For details on quantity purchases, please contact LifePath Press at 1-800-830-6270 or visit www.lifepathonline.com.